BREATHING OF
FIRST THINGS

Books by HY SOBILOFF

WHEN CHILDREN PLAYED AS KINGS AND QUEENS
DINOSAURS AND VIOLINS
IN THE DEEPEST AQUARIUM
BREATHING OF FIRST THINGS

BREATHING OF
FIRST THINGS

by

HY SOBILOFF

introduction by
JAMES WRIGHT

THE DIAL PRESS   NEW YORK   1963

For My Mother

Acknowledgments

Some of these poems have appeared in *The Hudson Review, Poetry* (Chicago), *Mutiny, Minnesota Review*, New York *Times*, Conrad Aiken's Modern Library anthology: *Twentieth Century American Poetry, Poetry For Pleasure* (The Hallmark Book of Poetry) and in Oscar Williams's anthology: *The New Pocket Anthology of American Verse*. Especial thanks are due Mr. Henry Rago for printing a generous group of these poems in *Poetry*; to Mr. James Wright for his deep understanding of my aims and extensive examination of my work; and last, but not least, to Mr. Oscar Williams, without whose help and advice this book would not have been possible. The poems on pages 57, 65, 88, 89, and 90 are from my previous volumes but all the other poems in this book are new.

H. S.

CONTENTS

II

ODDBALLS

III

LOVE POEMS

IV

NATURE POEMS

INTRODUCTION
The Quest for the Child Within

I.

JAMES RUSSELL LOWELL remarked, with half-concealed disapproval, that Thoreau described everything as if he had been the very first human being ever to lay eyes on it; and that this peculiarity gave his writings their most characteristic charm, although the same peculiarity betrayed a weakness in Thoreau's character as a man. But a man who possesses the miraculous gift of seeing things in themselves, in their irreducible miraculousness, does not thereby possess weakness. He is possessed by a power, and if the man is a poet searching for the meaning of his life, the power that may come to possess him is a moral one. It is the strength of his character, and it may well prove to be the source of his growth. Matthew Arnold discovers such a moral power in Wordsworth:

> *The question*, how to live, *is itself a moral idea; and it is the question which must interest every man, and with which, in some way or other, he is perpetually occupied. A large sense is of course to be given to the term* moral. *Whatever bears upon the question, "how to live," comes under it.*

Now Mr. Sobiloff, like Thoreau, retains the freshness of his vision, and he is still able—I had almost said he is still compelled—to see particular objects and persons and places as if no human eye had ever looked on them before. But something even more complex is taking place in his new collection. A poet's peculiar gift—which always has something accidental about it, something lucky, something for which any writer in his senses will offer up hushed thanks—here becomes the theme of whole sequences of poems. I am not referring to the book as one more among the endless imitations of Wallace Stevens, one more dreary analysis of a poet's own vanity, one more sterile series of nit-pickings on the theme of the relation between Art and Reality. Mr. Sobiloff's subject is not his own poetry; nor is it all poetry; nor is it some even more hideous abstraction. It is, rather, the rediscovery of the true imagination as a healing force. Moreover, Mr. Sobiloff's best poems embody, and also dramatize, the search itself; and they record the occasional discoveries that repay the poet for his gropings. They embody worlds of affection and joy that reward him by simply revealing themselves in their own existential fullness.

2.

Even the most cursory reading will make it plain that Mr. Sobiloff is not a "literary" writer. That is, he does not write poems about the books which he has read. I do not mean that he is "primitive" or anti-intellectual, like certain members of the most recent American school of the "noble savage" (that fantastic day-dream of hopeless yearning for virility concocted by prematurely senile eighteenth-century French intellectuals). The loud, public display of shame that one is literate; the lament that one's imagination is not coeval with the mind of God and that one's memory is not a wholly satisfactory substitute for the whole of human history —such laments and confessions are not among the flaws in Mr. Sobiloff's poetry. His imagination is apparently quickened into life by specific persons, scenes, and objects. The most successful of the poems are those in which he has been able to reduce the distance between the substance of the poem and the eye of the reader to the point where the poet's imaginative selections and emphases bring the reader's own imagination into focus. In other words, he is not a reflective poet. Of course, the power of intellect which did the selecting and emphasizing in the first place is considerable; but the intellect is self-effacing in the poems themselves. It is obvious that a poet may be "bookish" and yet write very great poems, as the example of Milton will show. But one of the most difficult problems in the study of Milton is to determine just which influences meant the most to him—one scarcely knows where to begin, the learning is so rich and alive. Mr. Sobiloff does not fill his poems with loving references to specific literary texts.

Introduction

This fact makes it all the more striking when a reference to a book or a writer does appear. In one of his "Prose Poems," Mr. Sobiloff suddenly evokes the figure of Walt Whitman, reclining as usual, dreaming, and "realizing that other people see the sky too"—a rather startling realization, when you come to think of it. As for other writers, in the poem "Wisdom" the poet has the following passage:

> *I warmed the hedge and alarmed myself*
> *With the hedge*
> *The clover I see—the pine tree*
> *And now worse than Wordsworth's Intimations*
> *Or whoever was in the poet's blind sight*
> *Like Keats searching*
> *Or Father Hopkins*
> *I would say as Shakespeare said*
> *To thine own self be true*

It is entirely characteristic of Mr. Sobiloff—especially as his character emerges, reveals itself, and works out its drama of re-discovery and self-discovery in this new book—that he refers to the great poets in person and not to their individual works or even to their literary reputations. Now, a reader might object that there is no difficulty in arranging a list of poets who are explorers of the imagination. That is one genuine definition of a poet. Of course, definitions of poets, like definitions of poetry itself, are likely to slip through the fingers like little silver minnows. Definitions of this kind, as Dr. Johnson remarked with no little impatience, ultimately reveal to us nothing except the limitations of the definer. Still, to call a poet an explorer of the imagination is as handy a characterization as any I can think of; and, if this characterization is at least tentatively accepted, then the reader may well go on to ask—as impatiently as Dr. Johnson himself—just why Mr. Sobiloff chose to evoke the names of Whitman, Wordsworth, Keats, Hopkins, and Shakespeare in the poems mentioned above. These names will do, of course, for they signify explorers of the imagination. But isn't the choice completely arbitrary? I think I may fairly leave Shakespeare out of the discussion; his very abundance of mastery renders him next to useless in a search for examples or illustrations for an idea, a poetic theme, or a school of any kind, simply because one can find almost anything in him; he undoubtedly had a single and unifying poetic vision, but the unity is concealed, or rather embodied, in a multiplicity of characters. Each of them is adequately equipped with his own imagination and intellect. For example, a reader must be willing to struggle with and define the full range and force of Iago's intellectual genius before he can even begin to understand what seems, at first glance, a very simple and obvious thing—that is, just what Shakespeare meant by writing his play *Othello*. Such multiplicity seems too imposing to be helpful to a critic engaged in studying other writers. Turning to Shakespeare for illustrations or guidance, the reader finds at last that he must accept everything or nothing. As T. S. Eliot observed long ago, Shakespeare does not lend himself to genealogies.

But it is not multiplicity alone that makes a great poet, and one may as well turn away from Shakespeare with the suspicion that his kind of abundance is a personal peculiarity which in itself is irrelevant to the critical problem at hand. But consider what we find when we turn to the other poets whom Mr. Sobiloff has mentioned: Whitman, Wordsworth, Keats, Hopkins. Even if the reader is willing to accept my rather whimsical elimination of Shakespeare from the discussion (and I trust it is clear that I am not trying to "dispose" of him as Mr. Eliot once seemed to "dispose" of *Hamlet* and as Shaw so often and unmistakably explained his determination to "dispose" of Shakespeare's entire production and to replace it with the works of John Bunyan), the real question remains: If one is searching for poets whose very names evoke one of the characteristic functions of a poet—the exploration of the world of the imagination—then why choose Whitman, Wordsworth, Keats, Hopkins? Wouldn't any real poet do just as well? Who is a more ferocious and exact explorer of the human imagination than Jonathan Swift? For that matter, why not summon up the mighty name of Alexander Pope, who is as intensely personal as any poet in our language and whose *Iliad*—though, according to that dismal old academic saw, it is "not Homer"—remains, for those who take the trouble to read it, just what Dr. Johnson said it is: one of the most astonishing productions of the human mind.

Moreover, the very suggestion that Pope had any imagination at all may have a certain shock value in these barbarous days when imagination seems so often to be equated with hysteria, when devotion to the heroic capacities of man's character through the images of Homeric grandeur seems to be equated with the mere listing of footnotes, and when correct spelling seems to be feared as a sign of effeminacy or even outright impotence. And why not list Catullus, Villon, Yeats, Campion, Raleigh, and many others?

The answer is to be found in the several meanings which are implied by each of the names Mr. Sobiloff mentions in his poems; in the context of the poems which include the names, the "Prose Poems" and "Wisdom"; and, finally and most important, in the context of Mr. Sobiloff's entire book.

Let us consider the names briefly, one at a time.

Wordsworth still has his enemies, and even his parodists; and no doubt he asked for them, if ever a man did. And I should add that, as a passionately devoted admirer of Dr. D. B. Wyndham Lewis's great masterpiece, *The Stuffed Owl*, I have rejoiced my way through Wordsworth's bad verse with the best of them. Nevertheless, I find it difficult to imagine that even the most case-hardened and parody-ridden reader of Wordsworth could deny the name of true poetry to the substantial body of his work which remains even after the most severe excision. As a poet, he is an explorer. But there is a further significance in mentioning his name. The particular theme which he explored in some of his greatest poems, and critically in the Preface of the *Lyrical Ballads* and in occasional prose writings elsewhere, is the very theme which Mr. Sobiloff struggles to explore and dramatize in his book. The theme may be called the search for the child within the self. It is a theme whose complexity is commensurate with its crucial importance in modern life, and it is so easily susceptible of misreading or misinterpretation that I will return to it later. Meanwhile, it is enough to note that Mr. Sobiloff evokes the name of Wordsworth not only because of Wordsworth's identity as a poet but also because of his great poetic theme.

As for Whitman, I should immediately point out that he is not merely mentioned by name in the "Prose Poems." He is shown performing a characteristic action: ". . . Whitman managing himself, Walt Whitman lying down, . . . realizing that other people see the sky too—think of it, the abyss is in the sand, shoveling, as a man should do. . . ." There is no claim made here for Whitman as a religious prophet, as an ancestor of the Beat movement, or even as the very great, delicate, and skillful artist that he often proved himself to be. This is just Whitman the man, and out of the image of the man grow two of his great poetic themes: his tragic awareness of the abyss that can suddenly open up under a human life and shovel the earth itself out from beneath the feet, and his joyous awareness that the miracles of the creation are beheld by other human beings, the discovery of whose existence is perhaps the greatest discovery of all. Mr. Sobiloff confronts both the abyss and the joy in his new book, and so it is natural that in his wanderings through the deepest valleys of his feeling he should have encountered the courageous, gentle figure of Whitman. Moreover, there is a further reason why it seems to me natural for Whitman to be evoked in Mr. Sobiloff's book. A reading of the very first poem in the collection, "Speak to Me Child As I Speak to Myself," will reveal the reason. Whitman is a various and experimental poet, and he explored a number of great themes; one of them is the struggle to grasp the immediacy of the creation with the honesty, freshness, purity of heart, and the unclouded intelligence of a child. Whitman's most beautiful poems on this theme are embodied in a style which he achieved only after a good deal more conscious experimenting and self-overcoming than he is sometimes given credit for. And it is in the style of Mr. Sobiloff's poems on the struggle toward the fresh vision of childhood—most impressively in the grave and free rhythm, but also in the remarkable images, unpredictable and yet perfectly clear—that the living influence of Whitman most truly appears. Here is Whitman in passages which are not too famous to enjoy again:

> *From the beach the child holding the hand of her father,*
> *Those burial clouds that lower victorious soon to devour all,*
> *Watching, silently weeps.*

Weep not, child,
Weep not, my darling,
With these kisses let me remove your tears,
The ravening clouds shall not long be victorious,
They shall not long possess the sky, they devour the
  stars only in apparition.
                        * * *

O to go back to the place where I was born,
To hear the birds sing once more,
To ramble about the house and barn and over the fields once
  more,
And through the orchard and along the old lanes once more.

O to have been brought up on bays, lagoons, creeks, or along
  the coast,
To continue and be employ'd there all my life,
The briny and damp smell, the shore, the salt weeds exposed
  at low water,
The work of fishermen, the work of the eel-fisher and clam-
  fisher;
I come with my clam-rake and spade, I come with my eel-spear,
Is the tide out? I join the group of clam-diggers on the flats,
I laugh and work with them, I joke at my work like a
  mettle-some young man;
                        * * *

The sharp-hoof'd moose of the north, the cat on the house-
  sill, the chickadee, the prairie-dog,
The litter of the grunting sow as they tug at her teats,
The brood of the turkey-hen and she with her half-spread wings,
I see in them and myself the same old law.
                        * * *

One need only read these lines aloud, and then read aloud the
following selections from Mr. Sobiloff's poem, to catch the tone
and imagery of a poetry which is never a direct imitation of Whitman but which resembles him as one rose resembles another on the
same abundant vine:

Speak to me child speak to me
You are learning
Yet you may teach me again the sweetness and the curdle
And tell me of the kid that is nursing under the sapodilla tree

And of the seashell I lost
And of those first scenes that I've forgotten

Speak to me of the innocence in the wading pond
That survives somewhere (I shall comment on the miracle)
Open your secrets to me
While I stare at your stare
                    * * *

Show me the buzzard ugly enough to die
The ground dove that has a hermitage
Tell me of the dogs that are better than cats
Cats cannot catch goats
Explain why that child is sitting by the road
Nodding and shaking and no-one there
                    * * *

I shall give you a biscuit
And let you eat it with dirty hands. . . .
                    * * *

Promise me child before you disappear in hide-and-seek
That your next step will be the fiction of this world
That when you leave the broken wall
You will keep your lizard spontaneities. . . .

Just as Wordsworth and Whitman are appropriately evoked because their particular explorations are similar to those that most deeply quicken Mr. Sobiloff's imagination, so the names of Keats and Hopkins suggest two great explorers whose lives and works embody, in one way or another, his own natural occupations.

The language of Keats is sensuous, as Mr. Sobiloff's often is. But it is not so much the style as the personal character of Keats that is most relevant to the American poet's new work. In the context of the poem where Keats's name appears, we find that Mr. Sobiloff turns to him, as to the other masters, for inspiration. It is not primarily a technical or artistic inspiration. The new poet is engaged in a search of his own, and he looks to the masters to provide him with living examples as well as the living precepts of their poetry. He tells us quite explicitly just what it is that he is struggling to learn: how to be true to his own self. And his entire book, particularly the opening sequence called "Speak to Me Child," demonstrates his awareness that the struggle to be true to one's own self involves a good deal more than the rediscovery of a childlike radiance and joy, though that rediscovery may lie at the end of the journey. The journey itself is a dark one. It is neither more nor less than the attempt to locate and reclaim those healing powers within one's self that are able to provide sufficient courage and literal physical strength for one to confront and overcome the agonies of the world which exists beyond the womb and which, for better or worse, does not happen to be shaped and arranged in a pattern identical with the orchards and rivers and meadows of that earliest garden, sunken now almost below memory and, whether wasted or redeemed, lost somewhere between the morning of dancing animals and the tousled dusk of sorrowing human faces. Beyond that garden we live a good deal of our death. We may insist on returning to seek it by trying to ignore the shocks and miseries that obstruct the only true way back home; and such evasions really amount to a mere refusal to live. The refusal, the negation, the despair—these are our constant familiar spirits in the twentieth century. They seem to be always claiming our souls even though we have not always made them any promises. But there really seems to be a true path back to the lost paradise, back home to the true child in one's self, back to the source of healing strength—back to the Kingdom of God which, we have been told, is within us. If there really is a true path homeward, then it appears that certain heroic men found it dark, sometimes yawning with dreadful pits of fire, sometimes winding and confusing and heavy with the whispers of murderers, backbiters, and the unseemly contorted apparitions of our own vanity. In short, there have been heroes on the earth, whose heroism consisted in their willingness to face the facts of pain; and their motive, as far as I can grasp it, was the motive of Thoreau: to front life openly and to live it fully, and, if it proved to be mean, then to get the true and genuine meanness out of it. For such a hero, the worst kind of death is to discover, when he comes to die, that he has not lived. And so, out of an abundance of courage and an eagerness to live—not merely to survive, as cynics and beetles survive, but to live—the heroes open their arms to the world as it happens to have been arranged when they were flung down into it without their suspicion or desire. Thereupon they discover what Job discovered before them: that agony and splendor often exist independently of a man's private whims. Even so, the heroes live on, they throw themselves head-long and live into the very teeth of the east wind. And apparently it is this decision which suddenly reveals to them certain resources of strength theretofore hidden from their eyes. Confronting pain, they discover that they are able to confront the rest of creation also, in the magnificence of its first wakening life. They see the world as Thoreau did—as though they were the first men ever to lay eyes on it. And they discover themselves and what they contain. After so many false starts, they are alive at last.

Now, Keats is one of these heroes. His poetry is only one sign of his courage, his eagerness to live, and his triumph in the struggle against pain and negation. The brevity of his life has nothing to do with the meaning of his heroic triumph, which is the essential part of him and endures forever. It is Keats, the heroic spirit, embodied in his great letters, which his name evokes in Mr. Sobiloff's poem: a fit model of a man who confronted and overcame pain and death in order to be true to his own self. Hopkins, of course, is yet another; and Mr. Sobiloff summons him reverently, calling him "Father Hopkins" and thereby identifying not the technical experimenter but the explorer of "elected silence," not the literary influence but the fantastically vital human being who filled his private notebooks with perhaps the most amazing record of love for the details of God's creation to be found in the English language, and not the recently fashionable non-Victorian manipulator of metaphysical conceits nearly as clever as those of the (abominable) Cleveland but the man who lived and wrote the terrible dark sonnets.

In each of these heroes, the search for the inward child is simultaneously the search for the life of the senses. Moreover, it is not an anti-intellectual search, not a primitive reaction against the mind. On the contrary, there is something essentially spiritual about the quest, for each man who most truly discovers the sources of radiance and feeling in the childhood which he bears somewhere within him, inevitably discovers at the same time a new power of reverence for himself, for his own physical being which God did create after all. Such powers as reward the honest search for one's self often carry a poet beyond the theme of childhood as such. Once the springs of true feeling are tapped, the living water may freshen the new experiences—and the new poems—of the man. The child is father of the man indeed. So it comes about that some of the best of Mr. Sobiloff's new poems are not about childhood at all—"You Cannot Paint Nature" is an example—but are successful attempts to confront realities, like the sea, in all their heartlessness, to confront them as only a grown man can do. In such poems the child and the man, the senses and the spirit, the strength of the body and the strength of the imagination stand together and support each other like lost friends who have found each other after all, at last, before death.

Meditating over the search for the inward child, I find myself suddenly haunted by one of the most glorious images of this search ever to be recorded in our literature. It was written not by a poet but by a novelist; and not in a poetic novel such as, say, *Wuthering Heights* or *David Copperfield*, in which the very language itself is made to glow from within with a happy or sinister light, as the landscape so often glows in the pages of Mr. Sobiloff's poems. No, the image of the search—indeed, of the discovery—which I have in mind appears in George Eliot's small masterpiece, *Silas Marner*, like a sudden and unprayed-for pinnacle of green abundance in the midst of a dark modern city, right in the very heart of a commonplace, prosy man, utterly alone, whose very fright, whose very greed, whose very rejection of his own life have been rejected by—by what? By some living presence within his own self. The passage embodies an impulse and a revelation that are so deeply at one with Mr. Sobiloff's own that they give me joy. In the novel, a defeated man unexpectedly comes home to himself, and lives again, if ever a man did. He is a prematurely old man; a stranger in the village of his dwelling; a miser whose gold, in what seemed the final viciousness of a cruel destiny, had been stolen from him; and so he is a solitary alien, a stranger among strangers; and he himself is the most unfamiliar of the common strangers he is doomed to live among. Then, suddenly, in a scene that is like daybreak, he rises from the page and becomes transformed. He changes from a single lost man into a type of many great forms of human life; and one of these forms is the poet who, like Mr. Sobiloff, contrives, somehow, in a world where all doors are closed, to open one of them and to welcome the living. And it is by this way—though he never dreamed of reward—that he discovers the child within himself. He is no fool. His gold was not his meaning. Moths and worms corrupt, thieves break through and steal, whether or no. There really is a treasure that men can lay up somewhere. Where? But a man must lose his life for the sake of love in order to find the way, as Silas Marner finds it. Perhaps the reader should be reminded that Marner is subject to cataleptic fits. The rest of the passage is self-illuminating:

> . . . Since the on-coming of twilight he had opened his door again and again, though only to shut it immediately at seeing all distance veiled by the falling snow. But the last time he opened it the snow had ceased, and the clouds were parting here and there. He stood and listened, and gazed for a long while— there was really something on the road coming towards him then, but he caught no sign of it; and the stillness and the wide trackless snow seemed to narrow his solitude, and touched his yearning with the chill of despair. He went in again, and put his right hand on the latch of the door to close it—but he did not close it; he was arrested, as he had been already since his loss, by the invisible wand of catalepsy, and stood like a graven image, with wide but sightless eyes, holding open his door, powerless to resist either the good or evil that might enter there.
>
> When Marner's sensibility returned, he continued the action which had been arrested, and closed his door. . . . [He turned] towards the hearth where the two logs had fallen apart, and sent forth only a red uncertain glimmer . . . when, to his blurred vision, it seemed as if there were gold on the floor in front of the hearth. Gold!—his own gold—brought back to him as mysteriously as it had been taken away! . . . He leaned forward at last, and stretched forth his hand; but instead of the hard coin with the familiar resisting outline, his fingers encountered soft warm curls. In utter amazement, Silas fell on his knees and

bent his head low to examine the marvel; it was a sleeping child
—a round, fair thing, with soft yellow rings all over its head.
Could this be his little sister come back to him in a dream—his
little sister whom he had carried about in his arms for a year
before she died, when he was a small boy without shoes or
stockings? . . . He rose to his feet again, pushed his logs together . . . but the flame did not disperse the vision. . . . How and
when had the child come in without his knowledge? He had
never been beyond the door. But along with that question, and
almost thrusting it away, there was a vision of the old home and
the old streets leading to Lantern Yard—and within that vision
another, of the thoughts which had been present with him in
those far-off scenes. The thoughts were strange to him now, like
old friendships impossible to revive; and yet he had a dreamy
feeling that this child was somehow a message come to him
from that far-off life: it stirred fibres that had never been
moved in Raveloe—old quiverings of tenderness—old impres-
sions of awe at the presentiment of some Power presiding over
his life. . . . But there was a cry on the hearth: the child had
awaked . . . Silas pressed it to him, and almost unconsciously
uttered sounds of hushing tenderness. . . .

"Speak to me child," writes Mr. Sobiloff, "as I speak to myself."
The child does indeed speak in these lovely new poems; and speaks
with the voice of the poet, speaking with awe, uttering "sounds of
hushing tenderness" to that shining face of our selves that is hidden
in the ravaged darkness where we have been lost so long. But here—
modestly entering one of the great living traditions of literature by
courageously exploring the abundant world of his own humanity,
and thereby suggesting the names and lives of triumphant self-
discoverers like Wordsworth, Whitman, and the rest—the poet
extends his hands to the child in the darkness; and, as poet and child
embrace, they look about them to see that all has grown light again,
it is the first dawn, the passing of time was only an evil dream, and
the poet has come home to himself at last. "Every door in me
opens," said Rilke, "and my whole childhood stands all around
me." All his past gestures of love were not vain after all, for they
have been laid up within his own heart and have formed his

character. Since Mr. Sobiloff's search is Wordsworthian, it is fitting to close this brief introduction with some words of that great poet which very well describe what the poet finds at the end of his quest:

> *. . . feelings too*
> *Of unremembered pleasures; such, perhaps,*
> *As have no slight or trivial influence*
> *On that best portion of a good man's life,*
> *His little, nameless, unremembered acts*
> *Of kindness and of love.*
>
>   * * James Wright

BREATHING OF
FIRST THINGS

I
SPEAK TO ME CHILD

SPEAK TO ME CHILD
AS I SPEAK TO MYSELF

Speak to me child speak to me
You are learning
Yet you may teach me again the sweetness and the curdle
And tell me of the kid that is nursing under the sapodilla tree
And of the seashell I lost
And of those first scenes that I've forgotten

Speak to me of the innocence in the wading pond
That survives somewhere (I shall comment on the miracle)
Open your secrets to me
While I stare at your stare
The wisest anywhere

Your reply to the world's dare
Is to fly your kite so high
Hanging to its tail through blown distances
To their laden inquiries you are like a flower looking
Or a cat roving

Your impudent silence pulses
Your smallest voice wriggles with desires
Speak of them to me
Speak of them and set me free

Your gladness flows
And I am thirsty for it
All my early syrups dried in the burning race
Leaving my lips no potion of their own

Child tell me of your tears that quickly dry
Leaping from your frenzied dreams

To the half-answered why
Where nothing is resolved but play
Tell me your wish sitting at the edge of the well
Stretch with me in your small awakening
Tell me what you keep inside your cage of littleness

Show me the buzzard ugly enough to die
The ground dove that has a hermitage
Tell me of the dogs that are better than cats
Cats cannot catch goats
Explain why that child is sitting by the road
Nodding and shaking and no-one there

I shall give you a biscuit
And let you eat it with dirty hands
If you remember how you felt
When you first fell into the well
Or how your sister yelled when you knotted her pigtails
And she never told

Talk to me with your hands about Tesal who braids her hair
And Leana who lets hers blow to feel the air
And of her earrings
Which she screws into her ears to frame her face

Tell me why Livingston Roll is your best friend
Because he talks and makes jokes on himself
Laugh with me at Randolph's green apple cramps
And how he won the bad conduct prize

Mimic Mr. Rooster crowing
Or what the cat said when it played with the dog paw for paw
Show me how you crawled behind a flea
And snatched his bite
How you imprisoned it inside your fist
And peeked ten times a day
Then roamed the attic
And played *do re mi fa so la* on the spider webs

Relate to me the tales you cannot read
Build me a house of blocks with
Your disobedient pillars
That fall without farce

Tell me of your naked stamping
And the barefoot bliss that fondles fond apologies
Whisper to me why each sickness brings another kiss
From Mother who spies and spies
And sighs over the sneezing tragedy
From shoeless running on the wet grass

Promise me child before you disappear in hide-and-seek
That your next step will be the fiction of this world
That when you leave the broken wall
You will keep your lizard spontaneities
Pray with me you will make reality your toy
And the earth will bounce again
With your newest joy

SILENT LANGUAGE

A silent language
Is like sucking a thumb
What penance is there worse than flying back and forth
As if to say where am I now

As it is primeval
A young pilgrim wanders first
Is there a difference for comparison
At the end of the pilgrimage

Each time I go away
I set my clock for dreams
I make a cloud inside my tiny fist
And when I land I peek inside
Like a child
And like an old man
At the same time

NANNIE

Nannie Mommie stop stuffing me
Like a dollop of dough
With a runny nose

He acted like a parakeet
Until the last snap
And then he ate

Speak to me child
Of the lull of the boat you play in
In your summer cellar

FRAGMENT—
CHILD OF MISCHIEVOUSNESS

Oh child you are of the richest foliage
Shaped like a ragged leaf
Your eternal measurement needs no intellect
You fall and run
Oh child of mischievousness
Who knows no evil

THE KITE THE CHILD AND THE SHOE

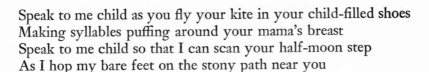

Speak to me child as you fly your kite in your child-filled shoes
Making syllables puffing around your mama's breast
Speak to me child so that I can scan your half-moon step
As I hop my bare feet on the stony path near you

My barefoot fable cannot stomach your small bow tie
As you wind in your kite strings
Speak to me child of your dreaming in a child's beginning
Crouched without ox-killing
Blowing dream breakers away
As the gabled ghosts spiral their ascension
Shying from the dawn's permanence
In your dream licking the day's fond wounds
And clawing at faith through your sleeping nostrils

Awaken child
Impress your juggling on your younger years of kite-flying
With your own hands that freckle the beginnings
In the extravagant fabric of your procession
Wearing too much happiness
Racing the labyrinth meadow through
Falling and picking up the strips of kite
Ripped and stuck to the barbed thorns
Oh child be in a hurry once more
Your bandy-legged pride weeps
Railed in by the meadow wheeze
Mocking at your bruised play

FRAGMENT

Speak to me child of your differences
The distance between man and child
Is a possible shyness becalmed by the impossible
They are relatives to each other—like Nicey a lovely child!
That skull is the same and the soul is searching for a morsel of
    thought
There is no expiration to childhood

JUMP ROPE

I look too often at my feet when I jump rope
I guess that is why I trip myself
Jane looks up when she jumps rope
And jumps on and on the pavement

My feet get mixed up when I jump rope
With one up and one down
I can't even jump plain jumping rope
But Jane can twist and turn
Hop up and down without music

Once I chewed gum to get my mind off my feet
Yet I could not get them together
I envy Jane
I like to jump rope too

Jane jumps in fancy figures
Almost like skating on ice
Jane is a girl and maybe that's why
But in my heart I know boys can jump rope as well

One day when Jane went away I practiced by myself
My one leg was ready but the other was too clumsy to me
I think I'll wait until I'm older

THEY BOTH LOVE ME

My mother baked the bread
My father pointed to the sky
And I the twig
Twisted on my mother's neatly pressed lap
While my father was distracting me
To climb the chimney

My mother bade me bow
My father taught me the pride of handshaking
Between the two I chose from each
And many times my manners collided

My mother bore me yet my father framed me too
He whispered and my heart leapt
She held me back and wove me fine
Their twisting tug of war
Kindled my restraint
My throat choked on her bunch of lace
As I tore the frilled collar from my scratched neck

When they untied one string
I bounced off their knees
And ran straight toward my woods
With my swaggering cap in my stride

And then I came to what how and when
My mother grimaced half-afraid
My father spoke of their likeness that I wear
And pointing to her said
That I came from in there

But as I grew I knew
That they loved fantasy as well as law
Each rhymed an heir
My mother with her righteous kiss
My father with his fierce embrace
Prodded me gently on my lifelong race

I AM OLDER NOW

Howard you are twenty-five now and I am fifty
But we remember differently
I recall when you were five and threw early pebbles on my screen
When your boy's longing was dripping from speed
As I stand next to you and nod my head as if I am listening
I am shaking inside like an old philosopher
I'll go home when I leave you now
And hum to myself some of the old ballads I sang to you then
I look at that twenty-five-year-old picture that I have kept
And see you still sitting on my lap and keep humming to the wall
I couldn't sing aloud to you now and you wouldn't listen

THE CHILD'S SIGHT

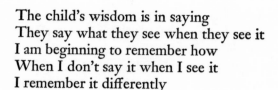

The child's wisdom is in saying
They say what they see when they see it
I am beginning to remember how
When I don't say it when I see it
I remember it differently

I am walking with the children
They have included me
None of us eavesdrops any more
We speak the same celestial gibberish
Our spirit ticks the same time
I feel again and am part of the inside world

The child is a little inspector when it crawls
It touches and tastes the earth
Rolls and stumbles toward the object
Zigzags like a sail
And outmaneuvers the room

I am learning the child's way
I pick up wood pieces from the ground
And see shapes into them
I notice a purple velvet bee resting on a flower
And stop to listen to its buzz

They have included me
And though I will not be put away to rock alone
And I don't roll down the plush hills
Nor spit for luck
I am learning their way
They have given me back the bliss of my senses

THE SCARECROW

In some things I am a child's size
Yesterday I hung around a brood on my knees
I felt in the circles
Made a castle in their sand
Surrounded two minnows with a wooden box
Winced and pulled their miniature fins

In some things I can only be lovable in a child's size
How else can I startle without toppling
Struggle their kind of impatience
And nag time into bowing

Nothing is more continuous than a child's first look
The beginning of shape with nothing to recollect
We had no need for thinking in our kind of play
Our images floated away the shadows
We shared the colors in the sky
And stood before the useful shell

We even brushed embarrassments aside
To betray some minor secrets

Then "Good-bye" they said to me
And to myself I said
"Oh uncomfortable scarecrow
Open your smile to the child's mind
Or the wind will drive you wild
Unstuff your tight-chested suit
And thresh away your awkwardness"

FORMALITY

Oh what is this to wear formality
While walking in the woods
This is not the child's way
To breathe in the living air

There are unnumbered things to be felt
And not to be thought
Smell itself and vision too
All the intuitions that can inform us

Here are the immensities of my child heritage
Here is where my curiosities have fled
After leading me so far

I have shorn the curls of four years old
And lengthened my trousers too
But where am I now
After the endless transitions that I bore

My triggering instincts are streams
Preserved for endless splashing
Where in solitude I pursue the wiry riddle

In my endearing report upon myself
My emotions lag behind the alarms
Of some unfathomable pace
As if to compare a dispute of my failing skill
With the performance of a wonder somewhere

Only when I breathe the cooling brink
Does my whimsy keep

And my unfinished time touch beauty's burning forehead
This endured struggle is a calm embrace
That thrills at the sinking sun within me
And warms my scatterings

THE PIMPLY WOLF

The pimply wolf
Who is shorter than I
Wearing his short serge suit goes calling
On mama's friend's choice braced-mouth daughter

He trembles the door bell
With his acne flirt
And acmes his spirit toward her tick
And flirted her organdy skirt (acorn-acorn)

In the skies
With butterflies in his own insides
His bold stutter
Struts earnestly his modesty in front of the family's look

They eavesdropped their eyes
From the back of their sighs
Plunging so safe—so safe
Their whist-playing shoulders
Whisked their tabled knees toward "ah!"

Pimpled and braced
And face to face
They squared right out of the parlor front door
As they raced to the prom and prowl

His acne howled "hah! hah!" inside
Behind the family's rack
For her kiss
Her organdy kiss

And she curtsied away
From the family's weigh
And with the prim on her face
Crackled "oh! yes oh! yes"

MY UNCLE'S DERBY

I almost lost my favorite uncle
My father almost lost his older brother
On one balmy Sunday he dropped by on his way to church
For his weekly family look
My back was turned to the baseball game I was about to play
Hurry hurry I yelled to my sister
Throw down my baseball bat
In a fidgety way she dropped the husky bat
Down from the fourth-tenement story piazza
Plunk onto my uncle's derbied head
I ran faster than my roller-skates
Squirming in my nine-year-old frenzy
I was leaving home for the eleventh time and did not
Tarry for a basket lunch
I eyed each cop on the beat
Slowly walking by wondering was my poor uncle dead?
There were no radios then
I hid in my aunt's kitchen and with a mouthful of hot cookies
Began to think it all through
What happened to my sister I already knew
There was plenty of time to go home
My aunt promised me shelter for the rest of the day
Should I roam again?
I phoned my sister in a voice of disguise
And she yelled Ma—it's him and I had to disconnect
My aunt made no fuss
She said that my uncle was better but dizzy
And that his potato lump would subside
I just remembered—I left my bat where it fell
I hope nobody swiped it
I really don't know why it had to happen

The fellows will probably think I forgot about the game
But they had Neil's bat
I guess I was the only one to get stuck
I felt sorry for my sister
She didn't see my uncle and I forgot to yell Duck uncle duck
My aunt called my mother
I instructed her to tell Ma that I'd come home if they really
Wanted me
But I wasn't going to be punished for an accident
I was relieved at the request to return
And whistled as I ran down the hill
One of the fellows ran into me and stuck like glue
I dare you to ride on the back of Bill's motorcycle
No hands on a cobblestone road
There was a dime in it and a lot of fun and no one could
Call me chicken then
Of course Bill had to run right in front of my father's store
I looked up and there stood Papa's horrified stare
His pipe fell out of his frozen mouth
He couldn't even scream
I yelled Hiya Pop and stayed on
When the ride was over I felt too much a hero to worry about
A beating
The kids all cheered me as we rode in
I got the dime and well-fortified with the praise that
Really counts
I beat it home to Pa and Ma and my uncle was there too
I talked fast and told them how the fellows cheered me
My uncle was angry that I did not stop to help him
But his head was healing nicely
I wondered whether he would ever be the same again
Pa looked up from his book and with a very young grin
Shook his head and said My son how I envy you

BLIND BOY IN NASSAU

(Dedicated to my dear friend Dr. Jan Steele-Perkins)

He became blind earlier than any of us
He wore an unexpected gaiety neither pathetic nor resigned
His curiosity was clear as sight
I walked with his doctor through the corridor
"That is Dr. Steele I can tell his steps" he said
I watched him seeing with his blind friends
His inquisitive fingers kept asking questions about a new musical
    box
Looking out of the windows through the venetian slats
Unshy he asked his little friends
To describe the colors outside where noises came from
"What is? What is? he asked in his own country's speech
His excitement had an inner light
And almost like an ostrich raising his longer neck
Stafford stretched his senses to find out where the world began
Once on a plane he clapped his hands and lost all shadows
The loved attention seemed to dwarf his blindness
He was the sight-seeing hero on the trip
He helped me lose slim pity
And simplified the reality of being born
His translucent sense saw description
He mimicked the wild geese flying and knew the rosebud's name
His naturalness was laced with accuracy
His past was no obstacle
He imitated deeper levels
He chipped away at the darkness and chiseled an identity

STAFFORD IS NOW FIVE YEARS OLD

(To Dr. Jan Steele-Perkins)

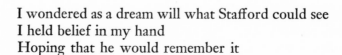

I wondered as a dream will what Stafford could see
I held belief in my hand
Hoping that he would remember it

Stafford lost one eye at one
At two he lost all his clear sight
And stored away his whole visual world
His index for recollection

Do you see the shadows Stafford
Do we both ask strangers where to go

Stafford reached out to see
He listened to noises like the outside
He wept without eyes—he listened without tears

I brought him two toys at Christmas
A music box to hear with
A cuddling cloth dog to walk with

I was not playing with Stafford's blindness
But with my own
Using my voice as a seeing echo
He reached my arms to collect his joy
Stafford led his imagination to listen to my face
To learn my name

MY HIDDEN FEELINGS

When my hidden feelings
Those hidden to myself become acquainted with my feel
Like a child finding its own infancy
A child the echo of a man
The small vanity that myself needs
Becomes the helpmate of harmony
When once I heed my need for joy—how little
Then I know the place within me fits the murmuring
As I look up to tiptoe on the creamy colors
That dissolve to earth in a smoky verse
The star—the glance—the blaze of sun
Illuminating the hasty architect
Best described passion washed away from heaven
And then to notice upon hitting earth
Where caterpillars' prudence nursed the moth into a winged
    butterfly
When once I retire my delight
And fate shifts its hellish visage
And my mortal eyelids close on this child's display
Then the inevitable ask of the grown-up questions about gloom
Oh no! The delights of mirth are not fickle
They hail goddess and queen
And play out the likeness of a dream
With soft or heavy hand
In the reality of the living or the slain
And the echo grows a pleasure of its own
And separates the ear to ignore the chains of babble
Sit and see the star proof of loving side by side

THE ANTHILL

Speak to me child
What are you saying playing at the side of your steady hill
Oh child did the ants follow you
They only eat sand
Did you watch them carry the ingredients for their establishment

Listen to their sayings
Pulling their caravan and carrying their long lot
The anthill is no sham
It is crouched and shaped by their instinct
They create a magical hill
And live under the snow now
And awaken on time
Watch them meander through nature's morsel
Oh neighborly voweled ants

Oh child did you scrub the ants from your hands
Your hungry time is near
You must leave their sandy harvest
And climb your own little hillside
As you run back to the family bowl

A CHILD AND THE COCONUT HEAD

There in the sand grew a coconut face
With husky brow and a white mustache
It fell from a coconut tree
Fell down like a man

Some great prowess grew him from a seed
Some windy footsteps grew him
Some great silence
A coconut head with sighs
And eyelashes running his face-side
Along his grained beard

This macabre skull feared beginnings
The milk still dripping from his head
Dripping down on green seaweed
Like white sequins blowing across sand bars

This is an old man I see
Crystals grayed in his wooden temples
In the white dying light
And crabs crouched bare
Staring at his stare

His shepherd's head was rooted in the ground
The grass waves peeked around helloing him
Then a child with little learning
Ran by and stretched across him playfully
Felt his coconut head and spoke of childish things
Stroked his beard and pulled him from his sandy nest
The hawks flew down from their vigil
Gawked and corruptly flew off
To find some dead fish head

OH JOSEPHINE

Oh child playing to sleep with your fingers in your mouth
Playing music with your toes on the bars of your crib
Speak to me from your inside
Why are you exploring me on your sulking thumb
Why do your open eyes giggle wondering what room this is
What else have you to do but grow bigger
Oh child you have found out so much
You are already as tall as a year
What is your measure—a tear for fun
Do you know what you see

WINDOWS

Windows surround a house
As children garner the frost

Their noses pressing windows
Their tongues sticking out

Windows garner the children
As a rainbow reaps the bereft

Windows surround the house
Their frames icicle the snow-beards

Children are in their cookie palaces
Peep birds chanting from their bare limbs

LIGHT STRUGGLING TO BE SEEN

Speak to me child—as I speak to myself
Light struggling to be seen
What hazy people cornered you in
Stampeded till you blinked
Speak to me of last night's ticking
Arguing out the day and years ago
Speak to me
Of the attic shadow quaking to be seen

What did you dream at night
That made you coward
Did you crush a dandelion and weep in bed
What dawned on you that makes you cower in the light

THE GANG

I came to grief and grips with a gang
Too early for my epitaph
Their leering leader growled through his stark blind grin
To strike me
Then signaled his tenderfoot to trip me up
I was a small potato and paled quickly
I lied
I told the gang my father died
Tricks only tricks I thought would work
But nothing helped they needed mischief then
They chattered their street-corner battle hymn
And chanted my nosebleed

They made me seem brave
Afraid to shiver I let only my lips quiver
Later groaning in the dark
And screaming pity at them
I learned gutter-wise
That cruelty is the tombstone of all boys
"Here lies and dies the body of a little boy
Without a penny to his name
A gang of little city fugitives
Killed him with names and sticks and stones"

THE BALLERINA

When I lost my childhood
Like other things
I trampled on the buttercup
Forgot the plain

When I lost my childhood
I reared my only ugliness
Until my fancy whispered rumor
That my beauty fell

I thought the city stacks had
Smoked my short-lived growth
Until when talking to my friend
I heard him say that years are never tears
But the little left to see

Then suddenly my eye caught sight of wind
Summered in a city yard
And within myself o'erflowing
Bearing my childhood back
Reaching with child's technique
I saw from my soul's back window
Surrounding the ballerina on the branch
The ballet of the leaves

MY COUSIN JACK

My father's father was a widower
He begat a brood and married a widow
Who had a brood of her own
And then they begat each other
The others
Then they begat the rest of us
There already were many kinds
So now Papa had brothers-and-sisters-in-halves

And there were favorites
And Papa's father picked up my brother
And dropped him
When he found his face wasn't Jack

SHORT HATE

They hated me because I was short
They hated me because I was weaned
They played with the spank-spank
They hated me because I was born
They hadn't even found out that I was two years old

They loved me because I was born
They loved me because I wheezed
It was your ancestor that crippled him

WHO WILL I BE LIKE

Who will I be like
The trash my parents defend me from
My friend the doctor?
What will I be like
The peasant or the schoolmaster
To what perfections confine
Shall I be myself
Ragged and uninformed
Twitching some menace away?
I am a yawn in my empty cellar
Swallowing a troubled breath

What will I become
An accountant of digits or dangers
Will I seem but a brain
Contriving a horrible innocence
For two husky legs
The other healthy parts
A heart that dusts my breath
And grinds my bloody stream?

What weapons will I acquire
What maneuvering words
A slingshot of anger that might slay my reason?
Shall I wear masks hold honors?
Shall I yield to the anonymous or the known
Transform the awkward crawl
Will I be bound by suffocating doubt
Or by an intricacy of glacial passions beyond predicament?
Convict my heredity or smooth its hump?

ON THE BIRTH OF A CALF

Oh calf—I am not ready yet—wait for me
Oh cow I have never been born before
What do I do
Lie still my calf—this is the path
I am not ready to breathe you out
Oh cow does it hurt to let me go?
I am too young to know
Is it light without sight outside?
Oh no see out there is the fence
And the grass is near

THE TWO-DOLLAR BILL

I was six when my mother first trusted me with a two-dollar bill
She sent me to the dairy to buy a quart of fresh milk
With the empty bottle in one hand
And my father's two-dollar bill in the other

I was six when I fell and broke my first bottle
I was six when I lost my father's two-dollar bill
I hid and I hid
But I couldn't find the two-dollar bill

When it was nearly dark
I dragged my toes home
To face my mother's stare
She thought I sneaked it on candy

She stared and she stared
Until my lung wheezed
I sneaked from my father's barrel
Into my little iron bed and shook until morning

When I could finally speak
I stood right up and said
"Mamma I fell and broke the bottle
Mamma please tell papa how I lost his two-dollar bill"

HOW DID YOU FEEL LATER

Speak to me child more
How did you feel later
Sitting in another place
Carrying your ways away?

Are the trees growing?
Is the sky clear?
Are windows near?
Speak to me child about what you see

Oh lagging behind child
What did you see?
A tent of boy scouts scouting out or windows?

The rattlesnake has a fang
It combines all snakes like men
Spitting smoking churning
Speak to me rattlesnake from your windows

How did you feel later
Without your fangs?
In a place snakes provide
Higher than grass
In what season user of time

A JAMAICAN CHILD

It has been so long
Since I've seen
A child's head
Soaking in a bucket

Mama soaping him away
His clean screams
Bubbled over on the grass
As they both held on

THE FAMOUS KITCHEN

Have you ever sat in such a kitchen
Where everyone sits and listens to famous music
Where the dog meal is on the kitchen counter?
Have you ever sat in such a family kitchen
Where all things are cared for
Endeared by old ideas
Have you ever sat at the end of an evening
With ice growing in the box and water near
A sponge on top right near the whisky
I have this very night
Looked through the panes
And lived a whole lifetime
Reassured by spoons and wet from tap water

EXPLORATION OF A CHILD—
HOW IT EXPLORES ITSELF AND WHY

First Curiosity:	Is that a fly Why is that a fly
Second Curiosity:	Where is that fly now Under a light like a moth Is a fly like a moth under a light
Third Curiosity:	Is that the water that I hear Why is the water there May I touch it Why can't I pick up the waters A spoonful slips through my fingers Quietly I stepped on the water Why I know why Old men do too
Fourth Curiosity:	Why does an old woman say why My doctor told me why His patient opened her eye Kissed his cheek to say Oh! I can see Is that a tree? When it was dark I've heard the bee But now I see Oh! Doctor is that a bee?

THE WIDOWED PARAKEET

Speak to me child about the white Parakeet
We call her Whitie the Parakeet
She eats drinks out of the cage
Only if you hold her in your hand
And when she is very hungry
She will grasp your hand

She will perch near the food
And she'll be eating seeds or drinking
Out of the seed and water cup

Bluie he's just more or less the same as Whitie
But he has male wings
Whitie will drive Bluie mad
She'll coo him so much
That it pushes him against the bars of the cage
Bluie will have to fly to the bars of the other perch
Because Whitie has Bluie in her squeeze

Speak to me child
Do you have more paper so that I can
Write this story down
I will get you yellow lined paper because
It will show up better

Bluie always comes to the cage bars
And rubs his chirp and sharpens his beak

Whirl is Carrey's Parakeet
Carrey says that since Whirl lost his wife
He has been rather timid
Yellow was his wife

And she pecked at anything that came to the cage
O Whirl your naughty nibble
Clings to the bar

One leg clings to my finger
But when it is good and quiet
I simply put my hand into the cage
And slowly put the feed cup in front of Whirl
Cupping the seeds in my palm
He bends his whole head down
And will eat out of the seed cup
He will do the same with the water and the gravel

Since Yellow died Whirl is not active
He talks about Yellow in a Parakeet's search
He does not mingle in his cage
He is half-chirping for Yellow
Wishing for her wing and her armless love

Yellow was born in 1955
Carrey thinks she died of old age in 1960
Because she never had a wedding ring
On her leg like Yellow
Whitie stretches out her wings as though to breathe
But Whirl clings to the bars
And flaps alone
He fans some breeze from the lovebirds on his right
From another cage
Bluie will drive down to get some cool breeze like a motor car
And then he will peck at the gravel
Whirl is eating now—he's hungry

JUICY MEANINGS

I have a wisdom now to know my age
Some years are gone behind
Some are thorned in front
And others reduced by love

Vigorous aging is no disgrace
I no longer stray my strength
Such is my mellowed modesty

My middle age is a festival
Of endless looking and listening
No funeral fantasy of fading flowers
But a rekindled kissing infancy
Couched in the softest glimpse
Of night near dawn

Throwing aside my colder learning
I have wisdom now to know my age
The tricky years have vaguely caged
My feelings in juicy meanings

My middle age has soundly brought me here
To gape to see the birds
Croak to hear the frog
It has taught me to loiter at a standstill
And breathe the lilies in the lake

In tedious lingering I stubbornly ripen
And reach into the sleeping immensity
For rhyme and wit
My middle-aged livingroom
Echoes coughing laughter and autumn poetry

POSY

Where did you get your colors my cat?
Pedigreed in an alley
Gray on lots of white
Orange ears with paws
Where did you get your colors my cat?
Your tail is lying down on your mother's floor
Posy your nose is like a face thinking
What is your mouth doing on the carpeted floor?
Oh well-fed cat blinking your ears
With your listening tail
The gray spot on your legs
Is almost the bell you wear
To warn the birds

THE SOFT GUARD

This child of one crawled the old way
All over the new airport floor
Laughed until she slapped the marble and banged her head
Then amazed in tears when her curiosity failed
She lay flat for help
Her sister about two-and-one-half
Fingered her own ribbon
Then with the strength of an elder
The soft guard pulled her up to a sitting position
And with small talk she mothered her own hurt lullaby

ROVER

Speak to me child as I speak to myself
What did Rover tell you as he died?

Rover was playing but I was too late
I tried to catch the ball but it rolled away
His paw bounced as the ball bounced away
He sprang over the fence trotting
As the street red light changed
Rover was caught in between
We both yelped
That man held me back but I knew
Rover couldn't get out of there
The man in the car didn't even look back
He'll never love a dog
They carried Rover and me back to the yard
To make plans
What else could I do?
Rover wasn't old
Our fun had just started
I lost him and never even found the ball

BOY CHILD

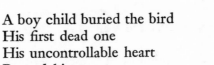

A boy child buried the bird
His first dead one
His uncontrollable heart
Poured his tears
I waited with him
I sat until he was well wept
This was no time for consolation

It was late near dusk
When his honorable self-pity shook
And his talking gasps asked
"Oh why did my bird die?"
As he counted all the reasons
For the bird to fly

"There is nothing moderate in nature" I said
"You must play with the birds that are here"
(How quick I was to bury the dead)
But he prodded his mournful breast
Placed a marker on the grave
Murmuring "Good-bye my bird—Amen"

BETWEEN FLIGHTS IN AN
ATLANTA AIRPORT

Boys speak to me of your giggle
And I will giggle too
Is it the habitual rash
From one contagious laugh?
I saw your friendliness on the airport bench
Where there is so little for boys to do
You played with sounds and mimicry
I sat like a spy—and why?
Bridged my neck to hear and see the innocence of your glee
And learned to abandon the obstacles that were confining me
Suddenly you popped up a marble a jack and a bouncing rubber
    ball
And then you noticed me
And we played—all three
Oh how your technique baffled me
My awkwardness palpitated in your realities
Suddenly the warning voice over the loud-speaker
Announced my time for flying into infinity

CHILDHOOD FORTRESS

Is the world of childhood a fortress and bold
Oh breathless child
How do I feel your world
I watched all day and ran behind the rabbits
I peeked behind your forever ruin
Your candy coal mine
And saw you returning on the happiest route
Laughing in your young back yard
Am I younger than Rip Van Winkle?
Older than you?
Before I depart help me awaken my tiny memory
And unwind my first watch
Oh help me recollect my sleepy truth

MEMORANDUM—
WHEN I PUT THREE FILMS TOGETHER—
AS ONE FILM

Now I lead you from Montauk's infinity to the City's mortality
And then I will lead you into the wellspring of the children's
    fantasies
Where infinity begins
I have brought you to the wildflowers growing at the beach's edge
To the seaweed floating ashore
I walked with you on the patches of sand
Up the cliff path
And raised your eyes to the skies

Now I bring to this periphery
The mortal ballad of a city with its stakes its railroads
With its alleys and stone hiding places
Into the breathing-space of Central Park
Where the remaining trees and grass are preserved
And where play can still be played
And where animals two of a kind can be seen in their cages
To where when I ran from the mechanical valley
Ran as fast as my feet
To find a child to speak to
I cried out "Speak to me Child"
The child replied "Mr. Man what shall I say?"

AM I TOO OLD
TO PLAY WITH BLOCKS

Am I too old to play with blocks
Too old to run my kite
Through the prisms of my own defeat

Am I unconquered by an untrue discipline
That silences the birds in the fields
And shames my gentleness

Oh what a mechanical valley is my middle age
A city automaton huddled in greedy speed
My heigh-ho is harassed by ambition
Successful living gurgles my rasp

Can I still lift my unfinished age
To run barefoot
Wave the clouds
And walk the muddy swamp to pick her lilies
Can I lie down in the woods again
And look up to wish

I'll hear the true sounds there
I'll join my senses with nature's smell
And journey with the sea

I'll touch love and wade the shallow rivers
Scan pick the rocks
Lie flat in my dinghy and listen to boat talk

I'll walk warmly in the winter freeze
Crunch the first white snow
And whistle my reply

No I will not sit into the fireplace
Burning bitterness time and tomorrow
While the cat's paw scratches the rug

I'll outstare instead its steel-green eyes
Stretch slap the mosquito
And lie back in the symphony
Of myself's sweet seeds

HANS CHRISTIAN ANDERSEN
IN CENTRAL PARK

O statue stand still
Your arms are filled with children
Whose lollipop fingers stick to you

The artist's hand brought your soul back to stay
He gave your face a weathered brow
Made your limbs relax and set you down

Your wisdom lives in a park where children play
Where boats float under lost balloons
Miniatures floating in children's ideas of safety

Hans Andersen they run to your homage
Full of warm noises
In a language of bubble and gum

They fondle your face with noses running
See you through the transparent lake
And though you are bronzed with age
They know you are theirs

II
ODDBALLS

FAMILY SCREAMS

Compare a stick with the wood
  Bent or round
Wound around a branch, or wet from a morning
A stock is shaped curved or rhythmic
Rolling like a stone
  It sleeps like the wind

Hear a stick
  It sings like a man
  Or hides in a basket
Watch a stick
  In the hands of a devil it makes sounds of hallelujah

Compare a stick with the wood
Compare a stick to the wind
  To a flower stalk half bruised by wind
Compare a man to his child
  Yourself to yourself
Compare a stick to memory

CRICKET

Some skinny people are fat
And some fat people are skinny
Are you dizzy abstract?
How can skinny be fat?
I mean skinny like fatso
Some fats are lean mean

SHADOW GRIP THE HILL

I once thought about the shrill sound of crying
Wondered how I would sound screeching like a child
I fondled the old man inside myself and throbbed my secreta
Wiggled my false wrinkles and grumbled all night
I awaited my magic tombstone

Why do you weep old man I said
Is it for the frisky life that you poked at
As though it was a half-dead fish
Are you hacking against the terrible change
Are you the bargain survivor of your age
Staring back at your honors
Are you recollecting the squeaky sharps
As you whistled through a needle's eye?

Of what failure do you tell as you wail and pray from your bosom
        deep
Is it forgiveness that you plead
Is this the meek answer to your solemn need
What fear do you strike
Will you be a nameless man
Will your shadow grip the hill
Will the natives forget your sins
Will your children bury your strange figure
What wall will your wail soak through?

Oh old man be valiant in this ignorance
Was your hand in dirt?
Let the herb blades sift through
Before darkness blazes into light
Your wailing betrays your little insight

Look up to the five pointed lights at night
At those stars that outstare you

Old man determined to die
Leave this hard job alone
And in this mystery
Behold a river swimming between the sweet rocks
Slipping down under the legendary sea
And sip your thirst hour by hour
From life's marrow
And let be what will be

SUN NUTTY

Am I an alley cat mooching a smile
What does a wheeze say to tragedy?
In two rooms I sat watching her tears fall
The horse fell the dogs whined
And all the excitement changed the subject
The horse fell when the cat noises were screaming
And people were running from the sun nutty

WISDOM

Wisdom has nothing to do with age
History has proved that
When men cannot prove themselves
On an aspen tree

Each person says to himself
Where am I
Am I in a jungle tree or am I a bongo jungle?
I am wood—I write I'm plastic
I write playing my piano
I'm wood I'm plastic
The scale—the scale
Like the scale of the fish

No more jungles and no more jangles
But for you the jangle
But to me the jungles
Under the aspen tree

I bring you my flowers
As my age increases in the plain fields
Speak to me child and
I will speak you back

I lost my hair but never lost my heart
I warmed the hedge and alarmed myself
With the hedge
The clover I see—the pine tree
And now worse than Wordsworth's Intimations
Or whoever was in the poet's blind sight
Like Keats searching
Or Father Hopkins

I would say as Shakespeare said
To thine own self be true

But what about me and the curate inside of me
Such a thing sings with humming feet
And the clover on the hedges
Will breathe you in
Prayers to be said
With no sacrifice

FROM THE AIR

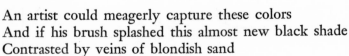

An artist could meagerly capture these colors
And if his brush splashed this almost new black shade
Contrasted by veins of blondish sand
It would be misbelieved

The truthful colors changed by wind and other particles
Blot my sight like ink
An artist could not capture the round mounds on these mountain
    tops
Or the curved lineage that nature made
And if he did the eye would scream at this abstract hand
Such blown shapes and shades are too fast for the eye
From the air I see the land patches spread their edges
And let the lakes through   .
And as I look down I tremble at such reality

SCIENCE OBESE

Logic is peculiar feel
Its stanchions stand like a cow standardizing instinct
Like a cow jumping over the moon
Logic is a peculiar moon gasping to be seen
A log-ship scarring Venus

Though the lute is stilled by man-made magic
We have solved no secrets here
Unmasked to earth
The moon survives mechanical measles

Science ricochets the timetables
Pencils the lunar prairies
A sparrow half-fledged on an electric pole

Logic is plush above a sky
And the robin wonders where to fly
The land sickly shrinks another settlement
Another typhoon of servitude

When the moon is won
Will it darken our planetary dreams?
Will our heart's temple our temporal bone
Make reverie in an ultra sense?

The lapse of gods dilapidates the lantern
But when the rocket is exhausted
What will our language be?
A leprosy of logic?
The tongue is tired
The planets glisten with diplomacy
The nightingale screeches an obese astronomy

ASTHMA

A weed can you make
A weed can make you old
One soft breath of littleness
Makes a pyramid fall
(And then like a stutter)
The object of the doll
Is not ragged
Yet filled with riches of love
There is a plant you cannot breathe

LOOKING BACK

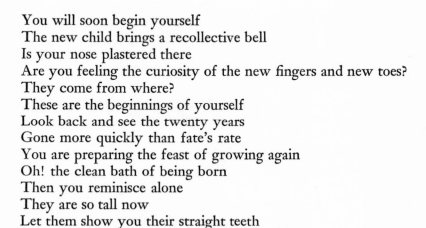

You will soon begin yourself
The new child brings a recollective bell
Is your nose plastered there
Are you feeling the curiosity of the new fingers and new toes?
They come from where?
These are the beginnings of yourself
Look back and see the twenty years
Gone more quickly than fate's rate
You are preparing the feast of growing again
Oh! the clean bath of being born
Then you reminisce alone
They are so tall now
Let them show you their straight teeth

MODERN CHANDELIER

My poetry is a legged chandelier to me
Not a match burning but a light looking down
An egg bulb embracing a word
It hangs from a chandelier and spawns in its own heat

My poetry is light gamboling with something I own
My mind my heart my soul

It strikes at me like lightning
A chandelier shaped like an octopus

This I felt looking up from
A dingy table under a late night
Embraced by a modern chandelier

THE SQUEAK ON A WHEEL
OF A WHEELBARROW

Poetry should not be a race against a race
At least mine isn't
Yet poetry is ticklish—an expression like the squeak on a wheel of a
Wheelbarrow
Almost as though the listener were a bird flying in its melody
Remarkably a habit

The same quality of sound that the oboe strains
The musical joint on a recitative scale
The triplet of a note sharp for nightingales
The key requires vision
The trombone bellowing retribution
The music squeak on the sentimental wheel of the wheelbarrow
Bound to ensembles
The emotional dream of emphasis delirious with song

STREAM OF UNCONSCIOUSNESS

The black cat on the white sand
　　And the green tree: Australian pine
A jet smoke (up) above (all) confusing (the) clouds
(And there near a wall is a vine) and there a wall grows a vine
　　　　improperly
　　Growing improperly
The sky is (man's) noise now
　　Blue and sometimes gray
　　Frightened with the ladder toward the sky
The job of love is never done
But there is Job
　　With more than all of us
The (climbing) ladder when it finishes speaks of shells
Black echoes in between the cracks offer
　　Like the fore to begin with
(Chimney is the ladder no larger than man
The log of humanity will prove the simplicity
　　On the sand on the tide on the grain on the whim on the land
　　With all fears that began)
Like a fly whisks in my eye
　　Like my ordinary hair that I take no time with
　　This is no mystery
My personal hope is a constant irritant
Granulated with all the bugs and sandals on the sand

LIMITATIONS

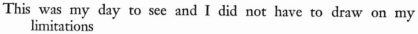

This was my day to see and I did not have to draw on my
    limitations
We nodded the blind could see and parted silently
I went to an airlines plane and flew back to my work for Monday
As I felt conched in this feeling I wondered why
The hero of the region had to roll his profile on the ground when
    I stood fast
Am I an iconoclast?
The blind who walk across with feet the young physique
Who throws a chance away yet wants to be young
The years never come afterwards
The relation between the eye and the ear is not the same
Stick your finger in your eye
Stick your finger in your ear—and then fall down

YOU CANNOT PAINT NATURE

You have painted nature's contours with so many eyes
With the dikes where the road is the dock
The subterranean city crawling in water back to the buoys
The lighthouse leaking for sight the water there
The bells shrieking reaching outside to safety
A ghetto of the sea brought back
The lighthouse man sitting on the reef overseeing the fog
Where the horn is the sea
What man did is zigzag
Deep in the sea and near the shore there is a tree distantly
The seaweed crowds sand wind prevails
The truest scene sea gull and tern
Two-legged birds of size preside
The dikes are the sea gulls a safety for their own protection
Men put them there against vagrants to live with the sea
A sea frothing indifference
You cannot paint heartless depths
Where the soundings unknown do not listen

DREAMING

The things I did not see
Fell out of my mind
The things I did not see
Whirled as I seesawed my head
Head swelled with a thousand patches
I breathed in thinking breaths
Short whelpings and whisperings
I breathed with my eyes closed
Feeling something rapidly lying in the bottom
Like the shepherd all alone

The things that awakened me
A dog's bark and my dreaming of his wagging tail
The last bleary melody that lulled me with her coverlet
Then stopped playing in the distance
Or the inside whining that stretches the flesh
Things I did not see
Far away from my human eyes struck at my tranquillity
Like the mysteries between disgrace and fortune

NEW YORK UPSIDE DOWN

I am looking at New York from the ground today
And literally I am face to face with the sky
Through a mirror on my window sill
I see a building upside down
A tree rooted close to the clouds
And a wall that I didn't have to dream through

The tree's branches were grounded in my visible back yard
Foretelling the bright weather
They are a riddle for such a day near winter
And warmed my bare feet through and through
The earth's slant of light built up within me
And leapt through the monkey ladder
An ancient fantasy for me to see the city fire escapes

My toes climbed and widened the winter landscape
I sowed my fixed eyes with an oozy and almost heady delight
I held within my vision the plain blue whereabouts of the sky
The painter's gleam would understand the excitement of seeing
    a tree upside down
And the clouds near enough to touch

SOUL'S RHYME

Plunder throws angels into serfdom
The world blows a typhoon of gloom
Where survival the missionary
Clasps hands in the prevailing mid-air

Earth's tumble empties heaven
The grave is skyborne
And bedlam's song a mousesqueak

The mountain's requiem ages echoes
And each ploughman wears wings
Hours roll out of their chains
And the substance of this new paradise
Is mad evidence

The spheres are unbound
Caves are not for hiding
The view is imprisoned differently

Yet somehow somewhere sweet truth marches our flesh
And the physics of that infinite shell
Will yet rhyme with soul

TENSE

I was sprawled out in a long chair tense and irritated
I waited for the fly to come back
Fly swatter and I patrolled a range between my eye to my toe
I really didn't want to murder the fly—my usual dilemma
But if he keeps tickling my chins I shall just have to protect myself
I swatted in the air a few times to give him a corridor to fly out
    through
But he with a fly's uncanny instinct
Signaled his swarm—and I just had to start swinging

WAITING

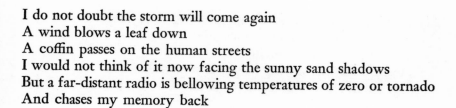

I do not doubt the storm will come again
A wind blows a leaf down
A coffin passes on the human streets
I would not think of it now facing the sunny sand shadows
But a far-distant radio is bellowing temperatures of zero or tornado
And chases my memory back

I REMEMBERED AND I SLEPT

My stumbled head cracked down on a flagstone floor
Spouting an estranged unconscious grief
I could not stop blood dancing
Or interrupt the unknowing height of a terrible flight
Patience careful blood unlocking the pores of light

Volunteer strangers pounded the country road
Quenching my sins
The speed of an ambulance burning the country silence
I lay flat—murmured raining froth white with grief
Friends as parents sponged the details of death
Oh how they laid my eyelashes down
I not knowing how I twisted
Who else was there? Whose fingers softened my words to save my
     breath?
And when I awoke one hand felt my flesh
Whose hand? My hand undertaking the examination of shadow
     and change
I lay motionless in the pulse of immobility
I was hearing my breathing
My eyes crept from wall to wall
My ears were waiting for their voices

The half-morning certainty made no masquerade
And rumor stretched its love
My feet and I an image bedridden half-faded startled from a
     punished sleep
Oh my arms again one suckling in love's blood
As the other patted my side my spirit recognized
I waited for the wound to whine

They wheeled me in the ward where other tender limbs joined
    mine
My ears like a mirror seeing heard the indulging smiles of other
    families
Half false half true
As the sufferers nibbled this round crumb
The fortunate sounds of nurses carrying bloods
For the doctor standing by to inject a good pain
To make the heart breathe
Then my cleft tongue wet my swallow and I remembered and I
    slept
I knew that someone's patient blood poured back
That this spectacular love would live transfused

A TONGUE'S TICKLE

A tongue's tickle is tickling inside me
Pent up to spring out
To spring like water
A tongue's trickle clogged
Like a small log inside my spring

This trickle is not a myth
But a deflection from direction
Made up of the immaculate harms
That I wish away and wish for
On my shattered pillow
In my insolent forgetting

All piled up like bedrock in my toe
These trickles make my heart
Unmanageable to my brain
Intermixing errors and questions of constancy

A tongue's trickle is reveling inside me
And someone is listening to its joyous spring
Someone thirsting impatience prepares love's breast for sleep

ELEGY TO MY DEAD COUSIN

My cousin Sara Preblod and I
Played in nearby carriages
With dolls dangling between us
When distress sneaked a smothering veil
Onto our carriage top

She died
I stood not even twelve
At the family street corner
Weeping faster than the rain
I saw a white coffin child's size prepared for her
I have endured the street corner scene in my childhood
Battle
Sara Preblod died at her fingered piano
As I held her music in my ear
At first I thought that I had made her die
As though I pushed her under the carousel kiddingly
Because I lost the golden ring
Going round and round
The doctor said that it was not our fun that sent her away
Yet such an inconsolable error is no solace for a child

At twelve I followed in the raining procession
I kissed her heart outside the coffin
And watched the wet smear the white pine paradox
I listened to the elderly murmuring incognito
The weepers said that she was safer now as I shook in dizzy
    opposition

I floundered in my day dream
And grieved my listlessness away to our secret meeting place
For one whole day I was victim too

I wrote to her and sent it somewhere far
I thought the thoughtless hand would grow weary of its vagrancy
And would listen to the echoes of my fears
And spare me such a poverty
This lawless cruelty could not gain my applause
I pounded the earth and blasted the silence with an infant's tear

O hear the human brain
Wandering on the watered ground
Twelve is too young
To see such milk spilt from a glass
She will be
You wait and see
Just wait and see

A GENTLE ELEGY TO SUCH A DOCTOR

John Herlin needed no fame
His acclaim from me is suddenly
His lighted life
There are these images
Himself face to face with his ideal St. Luke
When on one sandy day near his beach
I fell
His surgical shyness
Redeemed my malignancy
Weaned me back to walking
When sand sank his artery
Until his art (what's the word?)
He used feelings his art
That managed the flow and kept me alive
The nearby lighthouse
Illumines his rock-path cradled in the tide
As I cup up the spiritual waves
That mourn him his
Hippocratic fingers like Beethoven's
Inner ear played to my need
His fate all the mourners feel
That touch the ocean's bower and
Rip the reef—his shyness stems
Those tears that babbled on the ocean's
Forum. I am uttering the hope of my gray hairs
Standing with a fisherman's net
As a hammock
Searching for him—he is not here

PITTSBURGH

Near the road brim
Man's devil burned on the ground
His mouth pouring forth anger
In shades of white and gray
A tongue cracked and discolored
As earth stirred her iron ire
A thousand pots boiled raw hills
A spectacle of sparkling soup
Boiling bubbles popping
Bones and scars of stone breeding new giants

Man's devil dug in an open hearth
Melting mountains and losing ground
Witches writhed in gorged voices
Spreading phantom scars
Heaping screaming flames to the four corners
A smoldering canyon of melting steel
Patched their leaky skin, disguised their zinc faces
Only when the wind blew
Did the fiery cinders light up their secret eyes

Doomsday blasted with dynamite sticks dressed as Sabbath candles
Casting the rolling pilgrims into bronze statues
Targets for dumb boulders rolling down the mountains
Crust or ashes or late white smoke covered the clouds
While man's cranial fright plowed the old ground
And raked the quarry to stoke his volcanic heart

I SEARCHED THE SILENCE

I searched the silence for old sounds
For frost and hard sorrows
I condensed my triumph with a drink

Thought of curses that sharpened men's teeth
Of their swiftness and their unease
Their half-masted flags

I relived the seasons of my life
Saw the mockery that blocked my way
Like the wind on a thin day that ceases suddenly

Life was scarce and breathed without me
Sucked my greed into a trap
Made me forget my kinsman

I saw the secret of my falling days
How grief had paralyzed my freedom
And chased my loves under cover

SCHOOLMASTER

This was the first time I flew over my father's grave
It was then that I knew he was there
My father whose toil of limbs and mind and heart
Did father me

Wearing my autumn skin
I flew across tombstone dots
Where leaves fell to fertilize the future
In one process strangling and breathing
Now skeletons of truth
These graves were lessons I once knew

My father in his dying years shackled his younger promises
To the slavery of fatherhood
His hands unfolded bolts of cloth
Not for a shroud but for the doctor's fee
While I lay lonely yearning in my quarantined room
Not hearing his tiptoeing outside weeping
Eavesdropping for the rasp of breath

As I flew above my childhood among paths of autumn colors
I felt his anger-prod of perfection hiding in the wooden chapel
But could not hear the failing bell
Autumn leaves scattered the city macadam
And dusted my father's grave

My father was everywhere in still language
I flew above his grave and felt the dying flares
Signal inside me
The grave became a speck
Among trees rusting in orange age

Nature flew me across my childhood
While my son's first cry filled a new cradle
Filled me
With evidences that my father lived
Almost myself my father and my son myself

PROSE POEMS

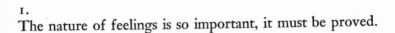

1.

The nature of feelings is so important, it must be proved.

2.

You cannot take inheritance and use it as a means to an end. The more comfortable you make me, the more impossible it is for me to see. But look at the half-moon in the afternoon. I have no magic about decency. With a baseball bat, think of it, softball, handball, it's like playing catch. What more can a furniture business sell? The second commandment talks about false idols. And that is the truth, in my book, in any Bible. False images have to do with me. Reality is a chair, and a chair is not wisdom. Glasses break— there is no reassurance in plastic; plastic is ersatz, it does not bounce like my bouncing ball. There is no replacement for a man. Like music running with toes, you will find a personality. Oh! then you find a sky.

3.

Imagine imagination. Impossible things have imagination have eyes. What is imagination is forever.

4.

The coat is not a colt. Like Whitman managing himself, Walt Whitman lying down, imagine such a dream, realizing that other people see the sky too—think of it, the abyss is in the sand, shoveling, as a man should do, as though it were to say: the coral is in the sand. This is not too shy to say. It grows imagination into reality. Mop up the floors. So clear with fear, just think how you would feel if garbage were not collected. I remember, at eight years old, in my rowboat, with no round oarlocks, when then and there. All the relatives and the friends, just themselves, made a pattern of their fear. They wonder about the sudden consequence which has no success but a lip uttering oh! a sigh. And why?

III
LOVE POEMS

ANNUAL SEARCH

The annual search for love began
Sailors chanted on their rum of the distant haunted cays
And once a milder crewman dared recite the moon
Leaving the land of trouble
He had found a different darkness there
Until he wrestled one storm through and found a beach alone
Where white patches framed the reef and coral palaces
Until he swayed feeling all the sun return
And listened to the crouching limbo
Under a long beached oar
Where midnight sounds reach out through darkness
The rocks dawn shadows the voice of a maiden's conscience
The sea that loves turtle and mermaid
The radiant lustre of long gone tribes
These are passions too

ALCOVE

Now as I glance at dusk inside the alcove
I see the structure of your loveliness
Your warm mouth chuckles love's melody
Your white-lighted brow sees across my lonely feelings
And carefully seemingly smiles to see
The fancy's hand that drapes your hair
So sheer so sheer
Now hear a poet's melody
Enchanted by this memory
Your white face is chiseled with feeling
A woman wears her gown
As her head looks down my sweet

YOUR BEAUTY
IS MORE THAN BEAUTY NOW

Your beauty is more than beauty now
Because it carries your hair between your ears that hear
You have insight clear through your beauty
I could not mould you better—how could I?
Your beauty set already your nod swinging to a glistening note
You have insight not so deep as not to weep
There are in the hollow of your cheeks
Your eyes that stare where mystery lies
Such eyes! delve in a deeper well than you speak
Oh ecstasy! the faster mind is careless now and not indifferent
To beauty's stead playing whimsy's stringed lyre
Your beauty is more than beauty now
Because it carries your hair between the oven of your eyes

LOVE

For my first time I held you in my arms
Twice I spoke surrender the day in my own way
Sailing through your hair
For the first time I understood the bare trees
Their waiting womb expecting buds
As though it were you awaiting me
Steering toward a cloud

MOON AND TREE

If she could be a tree (all over again)
With her hands and limbs and branches
Spreading out for me
If I could be a tree
With knotty eyes
I would look up further than the skies
And break through our balanced stare
Then stars would be my stepping stones
And then the moon would look my hunk of clay
Oh moon you have sent man astray
I've picked at your pock-marked face
From my child's balloon stuck in the tree
Yet in all my dreams
I never dreamed
That man would leave the earth for you

DANCE OUTSIDE MY SHOES

Your love has lived in you long
Longer than your sorrow
Your love is hiding in a periwinkle shell
Your love lives in your fingering

Sleep the blurry
Enough the terrain
Bring back your fingering
And the dancing inside your shoes
Choose the sun the sun again
Enough the shade

Tell me how I can open up my love
Back from the periwinkle shell
Tell me how to wipe my sorrow's leaf
And dance outside my shoes

I'll tell you how my dear
Put your fingers on my face
Or close your eyes
Until I tell you not too loud
In whispers of a kiss
I'll tell you how to bring your love from hiding
I'll tell you how I'll tell you now

PEARLS

My pearls died my love
They died for you
My pearls live my love
Serenely in their early shell
My pearls swell my love
Swell with sea smells and wet eyes
Pearls that drop down eyes looking down on you

THE JUMBLES OF MY FEELINGS

The jumbles of my feelings
What I see what I hear what I feel
The sky I am flying in
A high-heeled fly my cabin mate
And the jumbles of my feelings
Resist me as I cross this circumstance
From island to sky to city
The memory of rising and returning
From a distant place to here
In less than feeding time

On the descent the heavy breathing wings
Crowd all echoes and forbid thought
The locked-in laugh and spiderweb sigh
Suspend my ties between loved places

My dimmed eyes and clogged ears are mined by speed
While I watch the dimples in the clouds disappear
And the bubbles on the ocean's top lose their wrinkles
The drowned landscape lies too far away to see

Soon the four-winged craft will coast flat on the ground
Yet now right now
I drift to the motion-witted grandeur of my mood
The best of my feelings mingle softly
Hoping for the ride to end
To reach the other place

I love this rhythm in the sky
Pressing heaven's gate just before summer
But I need earth even more

My jumbled feelings ring out their earthbound bells
And face my face on the flat calm sea I am looking on
Recapturing the small consciousness
That reads the truth of place like prayer
This plucks silence from the fleshy screen
As the immortal cabin fly flies between

WINTER IS LEADING LOVE

Winter is leading love into a tough pathway
Her cold superiority is barren and balks the country cow
Yet inside me the warmest summer bee is buzzing
Of the merest chance to touch your wet unlighted track
In spite of winter whelps
The joy to see you makes up for sorrowing
And should your tenderness release your pride
I would breathe down on your bosom deep
How hungrily I would leap
Your steep lament
The angry yoke of discontent

LOVE BEGAN AGAIN

The love began again
With a pent-up indifference
Half ashamed of the behind time
That grew into unintentional longing

The love began again
A love tucked away from the quasi-real
The discipline that stayed dreamed-up in the helpless night
And grew those days back

Beginning love as a first kiss
That kisses on while the lips wait against memories
Love's leaning post
Going back to what it needs

The whispered look closed shyness
And left no place for signs
When once the love began again

SLEEPLESS FEELINGS

I adore your feelings
Because they are innocent
Nothing is empty

Sleepless I find your face
I climb the night like an unopened dream
Hanging between now and then
In the nude solitude

I adore your feelings
In your feminine field
You are a curious river
Fluid in your modesty
Your ribbed length of love

Your welcome is pent-up mist
Felt by the light of a nervous moon
That keeps the night away
From my disobedient heart

HAVE YOU EVER WISHED

Have you ever wished on a strand of your lady's hair?
Like seeing your love through a thin tree's branch
Have you ever wished without kissing your love's mouth?
Like seeing a kiss from an angry distance
Oh then how lips can weep for love
Oh my love I am wishing now on a strand of your hair
Where love's self is yourself there
Like the remainder of time
Blistering my swollen feelings
There where love's landings dwell
On a sea alone without looking oh my love
I am wishing through distance on a strand of your hair
And as I feel your coming back
I look down with eyelids closed
Fluttering nervously
Trembling the words—I cannot see my love

IV
NATURE POEMS

THE SEASONS CHANGE

In nature the meadow struggles and sips itself
Snakes are racked on their smooth bellies
The rabbit sinks in long grasses
And the deer rolls over in fright
Rage bleeds as nature screams
The damp meadow dries crisply
Unlatches her weeds and cackles her sounds
As the dust sifts the graves

The season's change whittles grass
As water bridges the dirt's imagination
The limp calendar strangles survival
And hides the worm in a brush meadow
There the strong language of secrecy
Grapples with the crack in the earth

MY FOG

The fog here is not so desperate
Because you can see the flowers
The fog is desperate and yet it flows
Like the porous finger
That springs the harp-strings
The fog surrounds us
Letting the birds out
And keeping the airplanes in

Fog
Stay today
So that I can play
And then I could say
That I saw a deer
This is when they can be
I could not find another way
So I built the fog
With my poet's blocks

LIGHT

There is a quickening to light
There is a sky where morning is a wish
A mystical tremor of elated knowing

There is a quickening to light
That rearranges unkempt circumstances
And daggers darkness with its justice

There is a quickening to light
That kindles pillars into prophecies
And quakes edifice immortalities
In watchmen's souls

In this quick light
Trees are idols
Moonlight is a window sill
And stairs turn into tulips

Quickly this light invents beauty
Kissed with subsided colors
Centered in an absolute
Kaleidoscope without monotony

WEATHER WISDOM

There is wisdom to this weather
The foggy droves of pillows and me
Listening to the windy hum of the horn
Near those hours of birth
Blinded with secrecy
A ferreting and for me unsure
Mimicking hymnal birds or the breast I'm seeking
The wrack in my longing
Tells me of living things and trembles me
There is wisdom to this weather
Upon the flat head of trees
When birds sing early at dream's window
Breathing of first things

FERN FAMILIES

Fern families are blown together around circles
Their embryonic features glisten like bird's necks
As the wind sometimes slowly waves their early glistening stems
Before spring fulfills the meadow
Nearby a lily pond cattails with nature's smokestacks
Keep a nightly vigil on the lily-pod's closed lids
There is no human caricature around this periphery
The small fern family cut down now by a house too big
To see the embryo
I poet plead for you

Ripping out nature's beauty is tearing up its roots
Watch nature misbehave in its hardest times malfunctioning
It leaves the pond's border free for me
To see morning lilies awaken unshaken
The strongest wild flower misbehaving here
Tackles her thorns in her very tangled nest
Near the wild grape leaves
I speak to you to tiptoe near and see
The fern around its circle
Kneel down sometime with quiet eye
Through two long leaves of grass
And wait to see the faces
Of cobwebbed nature cradling the meadow infants

THIS MEADOW OF BABEL

This meadow of Babel is love in a minor key
Sometimes I think it is the story of the velvet bee
Sometimes I think it's even me tugging the toadstool behind the
    tree

This meadow is love in a minor key
Almost like saying to the butterfly "Will you marry me"
Sometimes it's like the knot in the tree
Whispering spider set me free
Or the rooster croaking from thunder of the mouse squeaking a
    decree
The caterpillar squirms away from the worm
And watches the minnow turn
The cock robin sings the dirge of the meadow lark
And pulls the bell that peals for the fish that feels

This meadow is love in a minor key
Under the highest forest
Protecting the woodpecker chopping down the tree
The ragged storm blows the leaf back to me
This meadow is love in a minor key
Like the centipede promising mercy
And the grasshopper missing the snake's destiny
Oh musical twig blow away the witch that changed
My crocodile into the peacock
And lead the swamp back to the lily

HORSE LANGUAGE

*(Written from the window of Deep Hollow Ranch
at Montauk Point)*

The language of those horses
Is in the swishes of their tails
Their conversation nods and grazes as loudly as they are

Nearby the field a bird is flying the pond
Dusk is near
The fog dissolves into night

The language of the horses
Unbridled feeding lags modestly
A mirror of breezes fondles ripples on leaves
The fly and tick stand still and buzz a horse's hide
In their language of feeding

PARK

The muse is felt around the park
Spangling surprises
Ebbing toward fortunate man and bird
Who grow up an age here

Moments throb in entrances of the world
Resuming their discourse
Where ladies wait
Spreading wishes from benches

Museum heroes guide history there
And near the planetarium
Science tickles the moon

City cliff dwellers
Telescope the park's shades and delights
Basement eyes
Stare up from the manhole
All breathe in this air their mortal claws
Living between the perplexities of Central Park

The outside clamor crestfallen
Leads my flown fame
Towards petals not yet desperate
And leaves autumned with becoming

CITY TREETOPS

I hear a herd of birds
Chirping voices of awakening
I am curious of their voices
These sounds that trespass on my sleep
And turn me over

I hear a herd of birds
Trained by nature
Each flock evoking a city trait of shrill behaviors
Their spontaneous language overcoming the smoky noises
Of street whistlers of horns of footsteps

I look up to hear the scale of birds
Their lowest note higher than the treetops

FOAM

Foam wets lips
Sweats eyes
Foam
Light bulbs of the sea
Porous split by reef
Roamer of the tide
Salty blister
Fed by moisture
Bubbles and circles
Sprouting sprinting rocks
Their tiny eyes bulge
With seaweed bells

GINGER LILY, WHITE GATES, NASSAU

I had never seen a ginger lily before tonight
My friend carried her around in a green cradle
Fragile flower born in a strong thicket
Her round petals are shaped like plump eyes
They stare from a patched shed
Nature's womb expanding its high neck

Ginger lily buried deep in a swamp village
Growing in a swan lake
I had never seen the whole womb
Torn from its surroundings surviving love
The anguished root untied its stringy cord
As the flowers gazed from the swamp's dark mud

PIGEON EGGS

I saw two eggs born outside my box tin window
Pigeons wearing the city's deep abandoned height
Snow froze my eyes to see the fledglings sleep
I slept a pigeon father's sleep so steep
My own palm stood between my pane and their frosted wings
How do you rescue fledglings half-asleep?
The snow thwarted itself into moisture melting the snowflakes
I awakened to learn a pigeon's tongue
I winged my fright tripping as if to fly them back
They understood me and twice times twice
(Most the pigeons bear) they hatched two eggs
Automatically mathematically
But now I know how to unspoil them
I freed their trapped-in claws
And looked away to say "Oh fly
And some day wave your weathered jealousies back at me"
As though my wings were quickly theirs
Like sea gulls who leave and lead their flock
Into the poet's eternity

THE SPARROW AND A LEAF

I picked up a sparrow named a leaf
First evidence of Fall fallen from a tree
As yesterday I saw in her crisp shape an egg of Spring
The vision of an abyss closer than the sky
Where are we? Where am I? There is no safety yet
The cruelest boulder field gathers all the rocks
That people pick like empty shells
The jetty wombs the sea calms nature down to laziness
Tides can angrily return and safely raise the wind to
Horror sight
As people give the wind a name
I slapped the tree
I slapped myself to understand the cruelty
The lighthouse waits with wind and sound
Calls out its rendezvous
Banked on early rock as it isolates me

PLAYING BACK

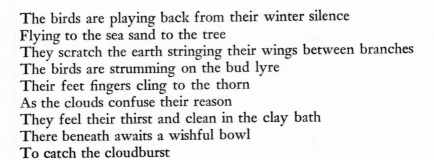

The birds are playing back from their winter silence
Flying to the sea sand to the tree
They scratch the earth stringing their wings between branches
The birds are strumming on the bud lyre
Their feet fingers cling to the thorn
As the clouds confuse their reason
They feel their thirst and clean in the clay bath
There beneath awaits a wishful bowl
To catch the cloudburst

CAVES UNDER THE SEA
AT STANIEL CAY, EXUMA, BAHAMAS

I had heard that caves are darkened ruins
Or where the bear or fox hides
But yesterday man
Tempted me to caves under the sea
I dressed in fish uniform
And swam wisely through crags
To pews of rock and organ shapes of limestone

In an aquatic cathedral
I sang out hallelujah
As streaks of white light
Shone through a regal dome
Coral colors and tawny shadows
Dazed my silence into Ah!

Whoever would speak of land attics
Or man-made undergrounds
Should dive these chasm's arcs
And shout their assembled echoes

I did
I the sea sexton clapped my hands
To hear the echo rise to the resounding tide
The moist acoustics harboring it like seaweed

Stalagmites stalactites
Those worn icy candles made my reverence to the sea
And lit up the iridescent mystery
Plato's caves crossing history

NATURE BE KIND

The threats of the elements are against us
A tide too high a wind too strong
Death's frost—a hot hot sun
And even Autumn's crackling leaves
Yet there is some kindness on the earth
The fairest spirit within me kindling life
The honesty of a day like yesterday
When nature stopped trembling reason
Returned the memories to the sea
And many other lover's hells to me

The threats of the elements are shameless
From drought to locust
Their perpetual windy vehemence
Wrenches many a firm bud from her branch
But at least words can fall softly from a poet's lips
As he wipes away the gloom from dust to dust
And muses—Oh! from leaves to leaves

THE WHITE MOON

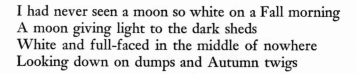

I had never seen a moon so white on a Fall morning
A moon giving light to the dark sheds
White and full-faced in the middle of nowhere
Looking down on dumps and Autumn twigs

My itchy eyes looked out of a small window in a long jerky train
I followed the frog's sounded fog along miles of awakenings
Suddenly like a photographic lens clicking at train speed
I saw a man on country horseback
A field asleep with half-sized cows
And a few gloomy pigs debating at the edge of a dry timid brook

Then night crossed the day
And the hidden tomorrow burst its large mock-orange eye
To break through the congested dark

While the starcolored stars still lit up the fog
And warmed the brackish swamp
A loud sun faced a white moon
Whose cheeks had just been powdered by cloudy puffs

LILIES AT THE POND
NEXT TO STEPPING STONE POND

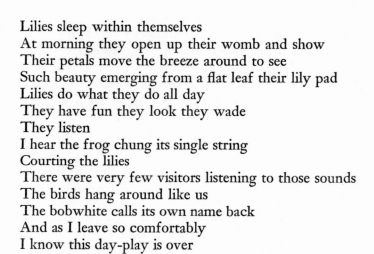

Lilies sleep within themselves
At morning they open up their womb and show
Their petals move the breeze around to see
Such beauty emerging from a flat leaf their lily pad
Lilies do what they do all day
They have fun they look they wade
They listen
I hear the frog chung its single string
Courting the lilies
There were very few visitors listening to those sounds
The birds hang around like us
The bobwhite calls its own name back
And as I leave so comfortably
I know this day-play is over
Putting the lid on my poem

WALKING FLASHES
IN ELEUTHERA, BAHAMAS

(Governor's Harbor)

When the rain finished
I walked barefoot and slid
I walked mostly with myself
Picked wood shapes from the ground
The moisture washed me
My sneakers made a pocket for the stones and pieces
I came upon some grass
And a lovely stone stubbed my toe
I hollered to the tree

I walked for myself
Saw such things that skies will tell
I gazed at heat colors
Sparkling firework tints
My eyes blinked at its stirring beauty
The things to see walking
Are too true
I held and smelled the grass leaves
Today makes sense to me
My feet are better
My heart is warm
And here I am